SELENA GOMEZ

Me & You

Posy Edwards

Introducing Selena Gomez

She's an actress, a singer, a songwriter, a charity worker, a fashion designer . . . and she's still just a teenager! Selena Gomez is a truly inspiring girl who proves that if you have talent and determination, you can do just about anything!

A STAR IS BORN

Born in a small Texas town in 1992, Selena went from being one of the kids in the crowd on the children's show *Barney & Friends* at the age of seven, to the star of hit TV series *The Wizards Of Waverly Place* by the time she was 15. And along the way, she has kept her loyal friends (including fellow star Demi Lovato) and family around her, and her feet firmly on the ground.

THE GIRL WHO DOES IT ALL

With her own clothing line, her own production company and her own band, she's a pretty impressive businesswoman, too. Her mother Mandy and stepfather Brian, who live with her in Los Angeles, help run her production company and help look after Selena's five rescue dogs when she's working. Awww!

BIG VOICE, BIGGER HEART ★★★✱

Known for always making time for her fans, Selena has shown just how big her heart is with her support for charities such as Disney's Worldwide Conservation Fund and UNICEF (the United Nations' Children's Emergency Fund) for whom Selena became the youngest ambassador. What a fantastic girl!

THE SILVER SCREEN BECKONS! ★★★✱

From child star to teenage TV phenomenon, it's truly a magical time for Selena as she branches out from TV into movies such as *Ramona & Beezus* and *Monte Carlo*, and scores smash hit singles as a singer, too. With more songs, more movies and more *Wizards Of Waverly Place* on the horizon, it looks like Selena's star is going to continue to rise!

Selena Gomez

All you want to know about Selena!

Timeline   Favourites   Following   Followers

Full name: Selena Marie Gomez

Nicknames: Sel, Selly

Date of birth: 22 July 1992

Hometown: Grand Prairie, Texas

First TV appearance: Aged seven, in *Barney & Friends*

Favourite TV show: *Gossip Girl*

Favourite bands: Paramore and Fall Out Boy

Best friend: Demi Lovato

Favourite food: Chicken with Hawaiian teriyaki sauce, which she cooks herself!

Favourite restaurant: KFC! ('Oh my God, it's the best food in the world!')

Strange talent: Selena can spit gum into the air and then catch it!

Star sign: Cancer

Eye colour: Brown

Hair colour: Black

Favourite actor: Johnny Depp

Favourite actress: *The Wizard of Oz's* Judy Garland ('Judy was the whole reason I became a performer.')

Favourite TV star: Jennifer Aniston

Celebrity crush: Shia LaBeouf

Fascinating fact: Selena was offered a role in *High School Musical 3* but turned it down

Rising Star

A star by the time she was fifteen, thanks to Wizards of Waverly Place, Selena Gomez started on the road to fame at an early age. In fact, since her mum named her after a famous Tejano singer, Selena Quintanilla-Pérez (known as the top Latin singer of the 1990s), you could say she was destined to be a star from the moment she was born!

FAMILY MATTERS

Her mother, Mandy Cornett Gomez, was a young Italian-American actress from Texas when Selena was born, while her father, Ricardo Gomez, was from Mexico. Sadly, her parents divorced when she was five. Selena grew up in Grand Prairie, Texas with her mother, who often took her little girl with her on acting jobs. 'My mom did a lot of theatre,' Selena remembers, 'and I would watch her rehearse. When she got ready for the show and put on her make-up, I would sit behind her and colour.'

Selena secret!

'I love to write, so you'll always find me Twittering or on my MySpace blog. I Twitter all the time! It's one of my favourite things to do – I love it!'

Watching her mum on stage gave Selena an idea for a future career. 'One day, I said "I want to be like you!" (to my mom)' she told *People Magazine*. 'My first audition was when I was seven. I was standing in line with 1,400 kids on a hot Texas day, and that was when I met Demi Lovato!'

AUDITIONS, AUDITIONS, AUDITIONS!

Selena and her future best friend were both auditioning for a TV series. It was *Barney & Friends*, a TV show for young children featuring a big friendly purple dinosaur named Barney, which began as a local Texas show and became a worldwide hit. Alongside Barney (who is a Tyrannosaurus Rex) there are three other dinosaurs: Baby Bop (a green Triceratops), BJ (a yellow Protoceratops) and Riff (an orange Hadrosaur) and a group of children who play with them. Selena played Gianna, while Demi Lovato played Angela. 'It involved a lot of smiling,' Selena says about the role. 'Singing, dance routines – nothing that's going to help me win an Oscar one day!'

BARNEY & FRIENDS ... ENDS ✶ ✶ ✶

Selena starred on the show for two years, but was asked to leave at the age of ten when it was decided she was 'too old' to be one of Barney's friends. 'I was so upset at losing my first TV job that I cried,' she remembers. 'I'm fully aware all this could be taken away from me in the blink of an eye, which is why I have the attitude of being grateful for every single day.'

She was also worried that leaving *Barney & Friends* would mean losing touch with Demi. 'As soon as Barney was over, I cried my eyes out because I thought I wasn't going to see Demi as much. So our parents decided to home-school us together.'

Selena secret!

When Selena was at school, she was made fun of by the other children for appearing in kids' show Barney & Friends. 'I still enjoyed acting, so I didn't let that stop me!' she says.

SPY KIDS!

After leaving the big purple dinosaur behind, Selena's career went from strength to strength. She won a small role in *Spy Kids 3-D: Game Over*, and in the summer of 2004, when Disney had a worldwide casting search looking for the stars of tomorrow, Selena went to audition. Three weeks after her try-out in Dallas, Texas, she was invited to Los Angeles to meet executives from the Disney Channel. They offered her guest-starring roles in *The Suite Life of Zack & Cody* and *Hannah Montana*, alongside Miley Cyrus.

RELOCATION, RELOCATION

With Selena's career taking off, her mum decided to move the family from Texas to Los Angeles where *Hannah Montana* was filmed. It was the right decision, as Disney offered Selena the lead role in a new TV series to be called *Wizards of Waverly Place* just a few months after they moved there.

ROLL   SCENE   TAKE

DIRECTOR:

CAMERA:
DATE:

It's written in the stars

Selena's star sign is CANCER

Born on July 22, Selena was born under the star sign of **Cancer** (only just – if she had been born one day later, she would have been a Leo!). Cancerians are known for being gentle and kind, and often sensitive, much like Selena! She shares the same astrological sign as some well-known, successful stars such as Tom Cruise, Harrison Ford, Tobey Maguire and Keanu Reeves, all of whom share the traits of being instinctive, hard-working and energetic.

Selena and the Wizards of Waverly Place

She had already made her mark in *Barney & Friends* and in episodes of *The Suite Life Of Zack & Cody* and *Hannah Montana*, but in 2007, Selena got the acting job that would change her life and make her famous the world over.

IT'S MAGIC! ✶ ✶ ✶

Disney was making a new TV series, called *Wizards of Waverly Place*, about three wizards in training who live in Manhattan with their father (a former wizard himself) and their mother (who is mortal).

Selena won the role of Alex, the middle child in the Russo family. Alongside her brothers, Justin and Max, Alex learns to be a wizard while keeping her family's magical secret safe from the outside world. When the three siblings have grown up, they will have a wizard competition to decide which one of them will become the family wizard and keep their powers, while the two losers will become mortal.

LAUGHING ALL THE WAY

It's a really fun family comedy, but comedy wasn't something Selena had really done before. 'Comedy definitely wasn't what I wanted to do first, I wanted to do more dramatic things,' she remembers. 'At first it was very new and very awkward for me, because the physical side (of comedy) and the timing are very difficult.'

She soon got more comfortable in the role of cheeky tomboy schoolgirl Alex, even though Selena says Alex is nothing like her! 'She's kind of mean and a little bit sassy and I think I'd get in trouble for that!' Selena likes her character, though. 'Overall she's confident and doesn't let anyone negative get in her way, which is a good quality to have.'

THE SILVER SCREEN

The show has been such a success for Disney that they have also made a TV movie of the show, with a second one being filmed soon. 'The movie was such an exciting project to work on,' says Selena. 'You get to see a different side to our characters. The TV show is all about laughing and comedy, and we keep that in the movie, but there is also more heart to the story.'

JET-SET LIFESTYLE

For the movie, the cast got to leave the *Wizards* Los Angeles studio and travel to Puerto Rico – where Selena ended up adopting a dog! 'His name is Chaz and he is called a "low rider" because he's got big ears with a long body,' she laughs. 'He's a mutt, but he's so cute!'

ALL GOOD THINGS COME TO AN END . . . SOB!

Back in Los Angeles, Selena spent the autumn of 2010 filming the fourth season of *Wizards*, which she announced on September 20th would be the final season of the show. 'I think it will be extremely emotional,' Selena told MTV News about the filming of the final episodes. 'I don't think they will have a live audience taping on the last episode on my request! I will be a wreck. Every day I go on set and see these people I have been with for the past four years and it really breaks my heart. It's been so much fun.'

17

THE CAST

David Henrie plays Alex's older brother Justin. Born in California in 1989, David began acting in commercials for Burger King and Quaker Oats when he was ten and won his first TV acting role in the series *Providence*. He then won guest-starring roles in hit series such as *Without a Trace*, *How I Met Your Mother* and *House* before winning a regular role in the series *That's So Raven*. He's pals with the Jonas Brothers and appeared in their movie, *JONAS L.A.*

Jake T Austin is Alex's younger brother, Max, in *Wizards of Waverly Place*. His real name is actually Jake Toranzo Austin Szymanski and he was born in New York in 1994. While you may think you've never seen Jake before the show, you will have heard him – he is the voice of Diego in *Go, Diego, Go*, and also supplied character vocals for the animated movies *The Ant Bully* and *Everyone's Hero* and a planned *Marvin The Martian* movie. Jake also appeared in the comedy movie *Hotel for Dogs*.

Jennifer Stone plays Alex's best friend, Harper. Born in Texas in 1993, Jennifer started acting in local theatres when she was six and won her first movie role in 2003's *Secondhand Lions*, alongside Haley Joel Osment and Michael Caine. She also supplies the voice for Amanda in *Phineas & Ferb*, and in 2010 won the lead role in *Harriet the Spy: Blog Wars*.

David DeLuise plays Alex's dad, Jerry. He comes from an acting family – David's dad was American comic Dom DeLuise. He also has two brothers who are actors: Peter (who used to star with Johnny Depp in a series called *21 Jump Street*) and Michael. Born in 1971, David began his career in the early nineties and has appeared in several TV series, including *Stargate: SG-1* and *Bones*.

Maria Canals Barrera is Alex's mum, Theresa, in the show. Born in Miami in 1966, she went to drama school before becoming an actress and singer. As well as appearing in TV movies like *Camp Rock*, she also supplies the voice of Hawkgirl/Shayera Hol in *Justice League* and *Justice League Unlimited*, and Paulina, Danny's high school crush, in *Danny Phantom*. Maria lives with her husband and two daughters in Los Angeles.

Lights, Camera, Action

Wizards of Waverly Place may have made her a household name in 2007, but Selena had already started on the road to screen stardom back in 2003 when she was just eleven years old, with a part in a blockbuster movie.

Her first movie role wasn't a big one – she is listed as 'waterpark girl' in the movie's credits – but it was in the popular family film *Spy Kids 3-D: Game Over*, alongside mega movie stars Sylvester Stallone, Antonio Banderas and George Clooney.

The story of a brother and sister who discover their parents are spies, it was a perfect movie debut for Selena, and her next role was just as enjoyable – she provided the voice for characters in the animated movie *Horton Hears a Who*, based on the Dr Seuss book of the same name.

MULTI-TALENTED!

In the movie, Selena voiced not one, but 90 characters, the daughters of the Mayor of Whoville (voiced by comic actor Steve Carrell). 'I voiced all of them,' she laughs. 'I had to change up my voice to do higher voices, then bring it down to do lower voices. All of the mayor's daughters look different, so I played many different characters.'

Selena didn't get to meet any of the other actors providing voices – Jim Carrey, Carrell and ex-*Home and Away* actress Isla Fisher among them – but she had fun nevertheless. 'I had never done animation, so I thought it would be cool to try something different,' she says. And she is a big fan of Dr Seuss: 'I remember reading his books like crazy with my grandmother when I was younger.'

ANOTHER CINDERELLA STORY

While filming *Wizards of Waverly Place* has taken up much of her time over the last three years, Selena has managed to find time to film a few more movies, beginning with *Another Cinderella Story*. Loosely connected to the Hilary Duff movie *A Cinderella Story*, the movie's director Damon Santostefano describes it as 'a completely new retelling of the fable. On top of that, it's a dance musical so it's really the comedy dance musical version of the Cinderella fable!'

He was very impressed with Selena, his choice for the role of Cinderella. 'She was fifteen (when we made the movie),' he remembers, 'and I'd never worked with somebody of that age who had the integrity and the self-awareness, the groundedness, the dramatic chops and a natural comic ability in my career.' High praise indeed and it doesn't stop there. 'She is a very, very talented actor who has really strong instincts and can sing and dance.'

Selena secret!
'Selena knows who she is, and I am around to make sure she doesn't change.' Selena's mum, Mandy Teefey

23

DANCING SHOES

Selena clearly loved the role of Mary Santiago, the young girl who lives with the domineering Dominique after her mother dies. Dominique is played by *Glee*'s Jane Lynch, whom Selena says was 'very sweet, nothing like Sue Sylvester in *Glee*!' Selena's character, Mary, dances in disguise with Joey (Drew Seeley), the school heartthrob, who then tries to find out her identity. 'This was the very first lead role that I took,' she says, 'and it's been very nerve-wracking for me. I had two months of dance training (for the movie) because I was awful! I was awful so I think it was really cool to learn.'

PRINCESS PROTECTION PROGRAM

Her next movie role, *Princess Protection Program*, teamed Selena with her best friend in real life, Demi Lovato. In the film, Demi plays a princess named Rosalinda, who learns how to be a regular girl with the help of Carter (Selena) and her family. 'The story shows what friendship really means and how it can bring out the good in you,' explains Selena, who was originally cast as the princess but swapped roles with her friend when they both realised it would make for a better movie.

RAMONA AND BEEZUS ⋆⋆⋆✶

It is her latest two movies, however, that have seen Selena go from Disney TV star to rising Hollywood actress. In 2010, she made *Ramona and Beezus*, based on the popular Beverly Cleary children's novels about a cheeky nine-year-old girl named Ramona (Joey King) and her older sister Beezus (Selena). She also filmed the comedy *Monte Carlo* with Corey Monteith from Glee and Leighton Meester from *Gossip Girl*. Based on a novel by Jules Bass, Selena stars as one of three ordinary girls on holiday in Paris who are whisked off to Monte Carlo with five-star treatment following a case of mistaken identity. 'I'm trying to make the transition into grown-up films,' she says, 'so I'm taking baby steps into more adult roles by moving from family to teen movies.'

With another teen movie (*What Boys Want*) in the pipeline, it looks like Selena's movie dreams are coming true…

Singing Sensation

Not content with just being a successful TV and movie star, Selena has also branched out into music, launching her own pop career. As the lead singer of Selena & The Scene, she released an album in 2009 called 'Kiss & Tell' featuring music she describes as 'techno pop-rock', filled with songs that reflected her life at the time.

KISS & TELL ★★✦

'It's what I've gone through with heartache, friendships and things like that,' she says. 'I wanted my fans to know me a little bit better after they hear the record.' Selena worked with producer Ted Bruner, her band (guitarist Ethan Roberts, bassist Joey Clement, drummer Greg Garman and keyboard player Dane Forrest), and songwriters Gina Schock, Tim James and Antonina Armato on the album to make it perfect. 'Because it was my first record, I wanted it to be amazing,' she adds. 'I wanted to find my sound and see where I wanted to go musically.'

Packed with attitude, the album includes tough girl pop songs like 'I Don't Miss You At All', 'As A Blond' and 'I Won't Apologize', which she co-wrote. 'Girls my age tend to change themselves for others, whether it's a boyfriend or trying to fit in with the "cool kids." This song says you are not going to apologize for who you are,' she explains. There are ballads, too ('The Way I Loved You', 'I Promise You') but it is the pop-rock songs that make her debut album so addictive.

Selena secret!
'I'm not at all rock 'n' roll, I'm so lame! My mum even cleans up my dressing room after me.'

SOUNDTRACKS GALORE

Kiss & Tell wasn't Selena's first musical outing, however. She had already recorded a song, 'Tell Me Something I Don't Know' (which she updated for the album), and had contributed her vocals to songs from the *Wizards of Waverly Place* album, the *Another Cinderella Story* soundtrack and Disney's *Tinkerbell* ('Fly to Your Heart').

'I have always loved music,' she adds, 'but to make a career out of it seemed scary. I focused more on acting, but now I'm putting more into my music.' She made the decision to work with a band rather than go it alone because 'I just really didn't want to be a solo artist. Originally I wanted the project to be called 'The Scene' but obviously that would be confusing for my younger audience who know me because of the show (*Wizards…*) and my name, so we decided to use both.'

The album was such a resounding success, Selena was soon asked to perform the songs live. 'I was so nervous, I nearly threw up,' she says of her first gig in 2009. 'My music was very new to me. But I have the best fans in the world, which helped!'

A YEAR WITHOUT RAIN ★★★

With *Kiss & Tell* selling over half a million copies in its first six months of release, it came as no surprise when Selena's record company asked her to go back into the studio to record a follow-up album, *A Year Without Rain*, which was released in Autumn 2010. Featuring Selena's hit single 'Round & Round' and 'Rock God', a song written by Katy Perry, it's clear that her second album is one she is really pleased with. 'I'm really proud of this record. It's very different, and kind of shows my growth a little bit in my music.'

Another chart hit, it surely won't be long before we get even more fun rock-pop from Selena & The Scene...

Selena Stylin'

She may only be 18, but petite Selena (she's 5ft 5in and a dress size 6) has already developed a recognisable style of her own. Whether it's designer gear, high street finds or her own designs, she always wears clothes that suit her shape and her bubbly personality! Read on to find out how you can capture her fun style...

DAYTIME ★ ★ ★

Favouring jeans and t-shirts when she is not working, Selena believes very strongly in dressing for herself and not anyone else, and hopes other girls feel the same. 'I remember how I used to dress a specific way for one boy,' she remembers, 'with my shirt tucked in, very formal, because I wanted to appease him. And boys are the one thing on every girl's mind!'

Her favourite daytime clothes are 'a plain shirt, with jeans or a high-waisted skirt,' though she's not quite as much of a tomboy as her character Alex in *Wizards of Waverly Place*, who is always wearing jeans, sweatshirts and sneakers (whereas Selena loves her shoes!)

Selena secret!

'If I could change the way beauty is seen, that would be my dream – every girl is beautiful and I just wish I could let them know that.'

EVENING AND ON STAGE ✶✶✶✶

While Selena is a bit young to be out on the town, clubbing or dining out, she does like to dress up for special occasions such as awards ceremonies. 'I definitely love to wear sparkly things,' she giggles. 'One time I wore a cute little black dress that was covered in sequins and on stage with the lights, it was so much fun it was awesome!'

Now she has a music career, she gets to dress up on stage when she's performing too! When singing with her band, Selena likes clothes that are easy to move around in, like shiny leggings and a slinky vest top, teamed – top tip if you're petite like her! – with high-heeled boots to make her legs look longer.

Favourite designers: BCBG by Max Azria, Georges Hobeika, Reem Acra

HAIR

Blessed with long, thick, black hair (sometimes given extra volume for a photo shoot with carefully hidden extensions), Selena's hair is heavily styled for her role in *Wizards of Waverly Place*, so she tends to tie it back on her days off to give her hair a well-earned rest from styling products! However, for awards ceremonies, Selena often blow dries her hair for body and then curls it into soft waves, or sweeps her hair up for an elegant evening look.

To get Selena's sleek evening style, make sure you condition your hair regularly. After washing, spray with a light styling product that protects your hair from heat and then blow dry your hair straight. Gently gather your hair together as if you were making a pony tail, then twist your hair upwards and pin in place for a sassy, swept-up style!

MAKE UP ★ ★ ★

Selena has dark brown eyes and a warm, olive complexion (inherited from her Italian mother and Mexican father), so she often doesn't wear any make up during the day, unless she is on the set of *Wizards of Waverly Place*. Her evening style is often smoky eyes with a pretty pale pink lip gloss, or sometimes almost-nude, natural eyes with bright red, glossy lips.

To get Selena's smoky-eyed look, you will need a pale brown and darker brown pearly eye shadow if you are blonde, or black and grey shadows if you are dark haired. Use the paler shade on your eyelid and just above it, blending it in well so it is subtle. Then use the darker shade on the outside corner of your eye and blend it upwards and outwards for a more dramatic look. Again, blend well, as Selena's look is not overdone. Then all you need to apply is mascara and a pretty pink or nude shade gloss, and you're done!

Favourite stores: Urban Outfitters, Banana Republic, Forever 21

Selena's style disaster: 'I went to a film premiere when I was 13 in a spiky belt and shredded jeans. Ugh!'

Steal Selena's style!

Selena came over to Britain last year (2010) to promote a special collection of *Wizards of Waverly Place*-inspired t-shirts and casual wear designed for George at Asda, but she has also been hard at work on her own clothing range called Dream Out Loud.

DREAM OUT LOUD

It's a collection you can imagine Selena wearing herself – boho-inspired dresses, floral printed tops, fun shoes, jeans, jackets and skirts that she describes as 'pretty, feminine and bohemian.' There's also something rather special about her designs – all the Dream Out Loud clothes will be recyclable, eco-friendly and made with organic cotton. 'I want pieces that can be easy to dress up or down,' she explains, 'and the fabrics being eco-friendly and organic are super-important.' Selena teamed up with designers Tony Melillo and Sandra Campos to work on the clothes. 'When I met Tony and Sandra, I was instantly comfortable with them and now they are like family to me,' Selena told fashion magazine WWD when the collection was announced. 'They are so creative and I love how I can just call them up whenever and talk to them about everything, even if it's just about changing a button.' Tony and Sandra are equally enthusiastic about

Style icon: her pal, Taylor Swift. 'The thing I can't stand about that girl is that she doesn't even need to dress up and she still looks pretty!'

working with Selena. 'She has such a good sense of what she likes and what she doesn't like,' says Tony. 'It was surprising as I've never worked with someone so young, and never really expected her to be that smart!'

UNIQUE AND INSPIRATIONAL

Selena has also added a unique touch to the clothes. 'The tags (on the clothes) will all have some of my inspirational quotes on them,' she says. 'I'm just looking to send a good message.'
    Unfortunately, Selena's designs are currently only available in the US store Kmart, but watch out for them around the world – hopefully they'll be in a store near you soon!

Steal her style: Both Banana Republic and Urban Outfitters now have stores in London as well as UK websites. Check out www.bananarepublic.eu and www.urbanoutfitters.co.uk

Giving Something Back

With a hugely successful TV, music and movie career, Selena is constantly busy but she still finds time to use her celebrity in a good way, helping charities that are close to her heart and encouraging kids her age to be more aware of what's going on in the world around them.

UR VOTES COUNT

One way she did this was by getting involved in the 2008 'UR Votes Count' campaign in the USA which encouraged teenagers (even those too young to vote) to learn more about the two men running for President of the United States, Barack Obama and John McCain. Selena helped to encourage more than 50,000 kids to learn about the candidates, and a mock election was held to show them what it was like to vote. Obama won, by the way, just like in the real presidential election!

SEND IT ON

Another way Selena has helped expand teens' knowledge is by joining 'Disney's Friends For Change', along with Demi Lovato, Miley Cyrus, and the Jonas Brothers. Together they recorded the single 'Send It On' for the organisation, which raises money for environmentally friendly charities. 'I'm learning about global warming and stuff like that,' Selena told Scholastic News magazine at the time. 'I've actually cried about this stuff because it's awful that it's happening. But I want to encourage everyone to help with that.'

Selena secret!
'I want to inspire others, help and make an impact.'
Selena Gomez

RAISE HOPE FOR CONGO

Selena has also found the time to raise money for a US children's hospital, and the charity RAISE Hope for Congo, which raises awareness about the violence that takes place against Congolese women. 'I'm happy that I have a voice, and I'm going to use it,' Selena explains.

UNICEF HERO

She has also become very involved with the children's charity UNICEF. In 2008, Selena was named their spokesperson for Trick-or-Treat For UNICEF, which encourages American kids to make Halloween count by raising money for kids around the world. 'I want to help encourage other kids to make a difference in the world and show them that Trick-or-Treat for UNICEF is such a great, fun way to get involved.'

The following year, when Selena was just seventeen, she became the youngest ambassador for UNICEF. Her first duty was to travel to Ghana in 2009, where she spent a week witnessing the conditions that children endure there – lack of clean water, education and healthcare among them. 'Every day, 25,000 children die from preventable causes,' she says. 'I stand with UNICEF in the belief that we can change that number from 25,000 to zero.'

With Selena continuing her campaigns with such passion, perhaps we can be hopeful that what she and UNICEF believe could actually come true. . .

Friends, Family and the Future

Because Selena has been appearing on TV since she was just seven years old, she's had lots of time to get used to living her life in the public eye, but she is fortunate to have family around her all the time for support.

HOME IS WHERE THE HEART IS ★ ★ ★

Her parents, Mandy and Ricardo, divorced when she was little and Selena's mum got remarried to Brian Teefey, which means she has three parents to keep her grounded! 'I'm very lucky to have two fathers,' she says about her dad and step-dad.

She lives in Los Angeles with her mum and stepfather Brian (who both help run Selena's production company) and the family's five dogs. 'Living with my mum helps me to be down-to-earth and to keep things real,' she explained to the *Daily Mail* newspaper. 'I consult them (her mum and step-dad) about everything I do, especially because my mum is my manager'.

DEMI LOVATO ✶ ✶ ✶

Selena is also lucky to have some terrific close friends, including Demi Lovato, whom she met when auditioning for *Barney & Friends*. When Demi and her mum and Selena and Mandy moved to Hollywood, they all lived together for a while! 'I'll be honest, I do have to pinch myself occasionally,' she says, 'I still can't believe everything the two of us have wanted since we were seven is finally coming true.' Selena and Demi are also good friends with singer Taylor Swift ('She has helped me through some really hard times').

For such a young star, Selena is already very sensible about her friendships and how important they are. 'I've learned who my true friends are,' she says. 'I've realised I should surround myself with people who make me smile. I have Taylor, Demi, and my *Wizards* cast, and that's all I really need.'

BOYS, BOYS, BOYS!

Of course, Selena does manage to make time for dates, too, though she doesn't like to talk about whom she is seeing. In the tabloid press, she has been linked to Miley Cyrus' ex-boyfriend, Nick Jonas of the Jonas Brothers, and although the pair denied a romance, Nick was reported as saying: 'She's an amazing girl, and anybody would be lucky to be dating her.' Awww. And in 2009, Selena's friendship

with *Twilight's* Taylor Lautner blossomed when she was filming *Ramona and Beezus* in Vancouver while he was there filming *New Moon*. But when she was asked if they were dating, she said 'I can't really say, honestly. I'm just glad to have a friend.'

In fact, in one of her more recent interviews, Selena told online magazine *Betty Confidential* that she hadn't been on a date for six months! 'The truth is, I haven't met anyone, but I'm young. I don't need to have a boyfriend right now.'

PRINCE CHARMING?

So who would be her Prince Charming? 'I want someone honest, someone who's very sweet to my family and friends, and polite to the other people around me,' she smiles.

THE FUTURE

So what's next for Selena? As well as the fourth and final season of *Wizards of Waverly Place*, there is going to be a second *Wizards* TV movie before we say goodbye to the characters of Alex and her family. Selena has the movie *Monte Carlo* coming out in cinemas, and she is also set to star in *What Boys Want*, a comedy about a girl who can hear men's innermost thoughts – sounds fun!

45

PICTURE CREDITS

All pictures courtesy of Getty Images.

ACKNOWLEDGEMENTS

Posy Edwards would like to Jo Berry, Jane Sturrock, Nicola Crossley Helen Ewing, Clare Hennessy, an

Copyright © Orion 2011

The right of Posy Edwards
the author of this work ha
Copyright, Designs and Pc

First published in hardbac
Orion Books an imprint of
Orion House, 5 Upper St M
An Hachette UK Company

1 3 5 7 9 10 8 6 4 2

A CIP catalogue record fo

ISBN: 978 1 4091 3249 3

Designed by www.carrstuc
Printed in Spain by Cayfos

The Orion Publishing Group's policy is to use papers that are natural, renewable and recyclable and made from wood grown in sustainable forests. The logging and manufacturing processes are expected to conform to the environmental regulations of the country of origin.

Every effort has been made to fulfil requirements with regard to reproducing copyright material. The author and publisher will be glad to rectify any omissions at the earliest opportunity.

www.orionbooks.co.uk